# Mass Communication, Advertising, and Marketing at the Strategic and Operational Levels of War

Where is the Army headed in the near future?  As questions surround the role of

Land Components in the now accepted Air-Sea battle[1] and while simultaneously fighting

for resources in a severely constrained fiscal environment,[2] where will the U.S. Army

focus? This has been the topic of considerable interest, even more so as sequestration

raises the possibility of even more budget cuts.  The Army leadership has discussed,

and is making plans for, deep budget constraints.[3]

It is in this context that the United States Army leadership is discussing the

"Human Domain." Lieutenant General (LTG) Charles Cleveland, Commanding General

of the U.S. Army Special Operations Command (USASOC) and LTG Keith Walker,

director of the Army Capabilities Integration Center (ARCIC), both spoke on the Human

Domain at the most recent Association of the United States Army conference in

February 2013.  Speaking in regards to Unified Quest, a recent war-gaming exercise,

LTG Walker stated, "the human is absent in our current doctrine, period."[4] He went on to

pose the question "Do we have a gap in our strategic thinking?"[5]  LTG Cleveland added,

"we're going to have to do something different to create dominance in the land

domain."[6]

To address this topic, working groups are currently meeting to discuss the scope,

dimensions, and even the definition of the Human Domain.  As of this writing, there is

no agreed upon definition in any Joint or Service publication.  However the most used

draft definition currently being considered in the working groups is:

> The totality of the physical, cultural, psychological, and social environ-
> ments that influence human behavior to the extent that the success

of any military operation or campaign depends on the application of unique capabilities that are designed to influence, fight, and win in population-centric conflicts. [7]

Why does the Human Domain matter? Capstone Concept for Joint Operations Joint Force 2020, which guides Joint Force development, describes how the Joint Force will "integrate capabilities fluidly across domains."[8] General Robert W. Cone, Commanding General of the U.S. Army Training and Doctrine Command (TRADOC) stated, "The central feature of the last 10 years of war is the importance of the human domain."[9] As the Army sees its' role in Joint Force operations conceptualized under the "prevent, shape, win" construct,"[10] the failure to effectively influence these environments of the Human Domain within the area of operations means the intermediate goals and objectives of the military campaign will be far more difficult to achieve, and will take much more time, blood, and treasure.

The military and diplomatic elements of the United States Government (USG) have been engaged over much of the past 12 years in population centric operations. Over the course of these years, lessons have had to be relearned even though similar situations were faced in earlier conflicts. It took the U.S. military years of fighting a World War II style conflict before adjusting to a counter-insurgency approach in Vietnam.[11] Although some units and areas of operation implemented counter-insurgency (COIN) methods, it was not the guiding doctrine during the early years of OPERATION IRAQI FREEDOM (OIF) and OPERATION ENDURING FREEDOM (OEF.) The U.S. Army learned through these engagements the necessity to engage with the population. It is not simply a matter of applying overwhelming firepower, but being able to engage with, and influence, the target audiences at the tactical, operational, and strategic levels.

Units and those organizations (non-governmental organizations, diplomats, etc.) capable of engaging and influencing audiences can be successful in accomplishing campaign objectives. Importantly, they can also prevent or mitigate adversaries gaining support among those same audiences. After Vietnam, the Army dropped the instruction of COIN operations from its schoolhouses, such as the Command and General Staff College, where the Army teaches its field grade officers in advanced military art. Because of this the U.S. Army suffered in the early years of OEF and OIF because the Army had to relearn COIN from the ground up. Although it occurred in pockets in both OIF and OEF, it did not happen from a campaign perspective until General David Petraeus led the effort to do so in 2006 from the Combined Arms Center,[12] and subsequently followed that conceptual effort with implementing the doctrine capsulated in the new Field Manual 3-24, *Counter-insurgency Operations*, when he took command of Multinational Force Iraq in 2007. It is in our best interest to retain the capabilities and knowledge built over the past 12 years. Failure to maintain these capabilities will inevitably mean relearning them again during the next conflict at the cost of national treasure, e.g. American lives and dollars.

> The air, sea, space, and cyber domains are all important and critical
> to success, but we can only achieve lasting strategic success in the
> Human Domain. Air, land, space, and cyber domains shape the
> environment in which the enemy will reside and therefore shape
> the human terrain in which our Soldiers and Marines will operate in [sic.].

But, it is through shaping efforts in the human domain that affect the

population, positively enabling us to effectively root out the enemy

and causing him to expose himself.[13]

When the U.S. Army is given the task of accomplishing USG strategic goals and

objectives, it must have the capability to not only dominate through overwhelming

firepower and military might via kinetic means, it must also possess the knowledge,

techniques, and procedures of addressing all aspects of the Human Domain in order to

achieve those strategic goals. "Dominating the human domain will continue to be the

critical component for success and needs to be a major priority for investment in

training, leader development, and materiel within the Department of Defense."[14]

As can be inferred from the definition of the Human Domain, all interactions with

audiences influence in some manner. These audiences are referred to as *target

audiences* and for the purposes of this research, target audiences reflect the individuals,

organizations, or governments to which the influence is directed. Interactions such as

military to military engagements, civil projects, humanitarian relief operations, etc., all

have an influencing function. The psychological environment of the Human Domain is of

particular interest for this research. The means to address the psychological

environment is through the target audience. Target audiences possess human factors.

JP 2-0 defines human factors as "the psychological, cultural, behavioral, and other

human attributes that influence decision-making, the flow of information, and the

interpretation of information by individuals or groups."[15]

This research is directed at what will be referred to as *influence operators*. The

term *influence operators* is specifically selected to ensure the inclusion of those that practice the art of influence in military operations, but is specifically meant to include Military Information Support Operations (MISO) (formerly Psychological Operations) and Information Operations Soldiers at a minimum. Influence operators are defined as those individuals operating in units or serving on staffs involved in planning and executing actions specifically designed to influence the perceptions and subsequent behavior of a target audience. U.S. Army influence operators'[16] goal is to impact the human factors of the target audience within the Human Domain. Current doctrine[17] provides processes to develop (a) the theme, which is the overarching topic, (b) the actual message for the intended target audience, and (c) the product, which is the message medium[18] to influence target audiences.  For example, the process outlined for MISO as a matter of doctrine is seven sequential steps: (a) planning to identify how MISO will support the commander's campaign plan, (b) target audience analysis, (c) series development, which is the series of products developed to accomplish one behavioral change,[19] (d) product development and design, (e) approval of the designed product, (f) production, distribution, and dissemination, and (g) evaluation.[20]  This and other doctrines require periodic review on how they may be improved.

Historically, U.S. Army process or technique improvements typically draw directly from lessons learned during and after a conflict or combat, as they should.  However, there is value in looking at empirical research from fields that may provide relevant parallels to practices used by influence operators. By reviewing this type of research, influence operators can benefit from the value of completed, peer-reviewed research, conducted using established social scientific methods.  This empirical research is validated by the methodology by which it is conducted, as well as the process of review, and the fact that similar studies reach similar conclusions, lending additional credibility to findings. Academic centers of excellence have often provided valuable insight into a variety of fields that the Army has accessed for improving its systems and procedures. Therefore, it is logical to review empirical data provided by academic disciplines for the field of influence or persuasion.

U.S. Army doctrine is drawn from "applied scientific and academic disciplines"[21] to provide current influence operators with a flexible process. Influence operators continuously search for ways to improve upon their processes. They do this to maintain pace with constantly developing technologies, social media, and persuasive techniques. Yet, there is a vast amount of data already available from academic research. Empirical data, such as that reviewed for this research, is constantly being expanded, and is available for review and consideration for application to the profession of influence.

Therefore, this paper will look at what research from mass communication, advertising, and marketing influence operators can adapt and implement at the strategic and operational levels.

Academic research

Academic research exists that can provide empirical data relevant to what influence operators may face at the strategic and operational levels of war and conflict. As noted earlier, doctrine should be taken from applied scientific and academic disciplines that have already pointed the way to extremely effective processes. Therefore, I wanted to move outside what had already been looked at and find a body of data that may not have previously been utilized. I looked at the disciplines of mass communication, advertising, and marketing of health related campaigns, all of which offer research covering situations similar to those influence operators may encounter when trying to change behaviors in the field.

A comprehensive, detailed search of the academic literature relative to this subject was undertaken. Comprehensive searches via EBSCOhost Service using the specific databases of *Communication and Mass Media Complete*, *Business Source Complete*, *Academic Source Complete*, and *PsycINFO* were used.[22] Based on the results of that search, forty-one research studies were examined, across a range of advertising, marketing, mass communication, and social marketing campaigns. The priority was to determine which applications have been successful, and how the Army may learn from them for possible application in operations abroad with foreign audiences. To find the types of research that may apply to Army or Joint execution of influence operations, I found the most useful data and most expansive range of studies in health related communication campaigns through keyword and database searches discussed above.

With the vast amount of information available across health related campaigns, the need to narrow the scope of research quickly became apparent. There was a need to rule out certain categories of research because they would not apply to a majority of potential efforts influence operators would execute. Listed below are the types of studies excluded and the reasons they were not used in this project.

Studies dealing with addictive behavior were eliminated because addictive behavior is unique. It has a biological component separate from cognitive functions, which are the areas influence operators focus on. The chemical dependencies associated with addictive behaviors are an entirely different aspect beyond what this research intended to review. Therefore, if an element's mission focuses on counter-drug/narcotic as it relates to demand reduction,[23] there will be a necessity to review studies that deal with this type of behavior. However, the majority of influence operations now can be categorized as focusing on counterterrorism, anti-smuggling, anti-trafficking, and good governance, with some counter-piracy and increasing amounts of military to military capacity building.

Studies conducted in clinical settings eliminated too many of the factors that influence operators would face in real-world communication campaigns. Influence operators do not have the benefit of filtering out societal or group influences that may impact behaviors and attitudes, as do clinical studies.

Studies that dealt with coercive techniques were eliminated. The situations typically faced in strategic and operational level missions involve providing convincing information in order to persuade the foreign target audience to make a decision on its own without the use of strong-arm tactics. Persuasion through coercion is not a viable means to impact long-term behavior and attitudes. Coercive techniques are successful until the coercion is no longer present.

This study is focused on elements that can be applied at the operational and strategic levels. Therefore, techniques deemed effective only through personal contact and interaction, while effective at the tactical level, were eliminated because messages and content provided from the operational or strategic level typically lack direct personal contact or direct interaction between the influence operator and the target audience. Additionally, the ability to utilize a technique requiring personal contact and interaction is unsustainable, cost prohibitive and, more importantly, not feasible in reaching a vast audience such as would likely be carried out during strategic and operational messaging efforts.

Empirical results from the academic literature

The first significant result is one that has been emphasized across many fields of study dealing with communication, and that is the importance of developing an in-depth understanding of the target audience, called *target audience analysis*. Intensive analysis of the target audience is an absolutely essential step for successful influence. Processes used by military practitioners, Madison Avenue marketers, or public relations experts, all will suffer without a valid target audience analysis, whether they use the RACE[24] model, health communication's MODE[25] process, or any other approach. Without this analytical step, the remainder of the influence effort is impacted. A poor target audience analysis leads to ineffective message design,[26] inaccurate media recommendations, and poor product design. It also invalidates outcome evaluation or assessment. As has famously been said, "Nations can blunder into war. They cannot blunder into peace."[27] The analogy to influence efforts is clear: success in influence operations is not something you fall into; it takes a concerted and deliberate effort.

Simply put, target audience analysis is researching a target audience's characteristics, habits, norms, taboos, religious beliefs, attitudes, and other aspects of the target audience that may provide insight into the way they perceive and interpret information. A target audience analysis should delve into how the target audience's behaviors are formed. Fishbein et al discuss the importance of evaluating outcome expectancies,[28] normative beliefs,[29] and self-efficacy[30] in the target audience to consider the feasibility of their accepting the message and the potential that they will exhibit the desired outcome. Messages targeting these three areas identified by Fishbein have proven effective, but it is important to understand that "behavior is influenced by [. . . ] attitudes, norms and self-efficacy" and "the beliefs underlying those psychosocial variables."[31] To increase the prospect of product effectiveness (in terms of leading to a desired behavior), those developing the product must have a detailed understanding of the target audience's vulnerability to the message and thus the potential to change their behavior. It is important to identify societal norms, and the likely impact the product will therefore have on behavior, attitudes, and perceptions.[32]

Understanding a target audience in terms of these specifics reduces the potential for ineffective message design, inaccurate media recommendations, and poor product design. It also assists in developing an accurate baseline or starting point that in turn provides greater accuracy for future outcome evaluations and assessments. Because target audience analysis identifies where a target audience may be vulnerable, it also makes it possible to determine by which means they are accessible, i.e. television, social media, radio, etc.

The second significant takeaway of this study is that developing a successful influence effort starts with solid behavioral and message design theory. Successful communication campaigns follow a proven process, but also are based on solid behavioral and message design theory.[33] The process steps[34] developed should be based on "well-accepted principles of effective campaign design and evaluation."[35] The process outlined in Noar's study as part of his suggested method listed a step that

10

should be considered for current doctrine: Step 2 *Using theory as a conceptual foundation:* a significant step in his process. This step helps to lay the foundation for the persuasive process by ensuring that individual/s developing a product are basing it on proven theory. Without this step, campaign developers can easily wander into the "good-idea" mode of product development where individuals believe they instinctively know what a convincing product is without doing the necessary steps of analysis first. There are numerous examples throughout marketing and advertising of this approach being taken, and the poor outcomes that resulted. One such example was the naming of the Chevrolet Nova, and the resulting poor sales in Spanish speaking countries where of course "Nova" translates as "no go." Influence by good-idea does not work, and in many cases can cause negative outcomes.

Using behavioral theory as a basis for campaign planning on the other hand provides a baseline understanding of the approach to be taken, and thus offers the opportunity to enhance message design.[36] Health related campaigns found varying degrees of success with these behavioral theories and their application to associated efforts. Greater understanding of these theories and associated techniques will likewise enhance influence operations.

Many of the studies addressed social norms.[37] "'Social norms' marketing assumes that once you correct the perceived norm so that it matches the actual norm, individuals will alter their behavior accordingly."[38] Social norms are often part of the discussion when dealing with areas such as human rights and the attempts by outside organizations or other nations to adjust the social norm and associated practices in the target nation toward a more accepted international norm. In the case of human rights, providing information to internal groups already anxious to cause change but in need of information can typically provide this information across the population via the "chattering classes," i.e. those who may initiate the topic dialogue and keep it on the air waves of public discussion in cafés, religious services, family gatherings, and street dialogue.

Providing accurate, believable, and easily understood information[39] from credible sources regarding the on-going public debate occurring outside the target nation to those internal audiences, who may not be privy to information regarding the actions of others on their behalf, helps in several ways. Two in particular are worth considering. First, there is the awareness that other nations are attempting to advance an issue on their behalf. This provides a realization that others care about their plight and that the expectations of an oppressed population within a target nation are acknowledged as reasonable from an international perspective. Second, the flooding of information into an internal population's knowledge serves to empower them against governmental rhetoric or propaganda, foments continuous discussion, and maintains the topic in the public conversation. In the case of the abolition of slavery, for example, American abolitionists were influenced by Europe, followed by support for abolition becoming a prevalent belief and subsequently spreading to Latin America.[40]

Several studies reviewed techniques of communication campaigns' which attempt to move a target audience toward an internationally accepted social norm. A number are associated with Daryl Bem's Self-Perception Theory, which asserts "individuals know their own attitudes, emotions, and other internal states partially by inferring them from observations of their own overt behavior."[41] The foot-in-the-door technique to modify socially conscious behavior is effective, therefore, because people use their own behavior as a cue regarding attitudinal dispositions.[42] The foot-in-the-door technique applies a gradual approach, that "entail[s] gaining compliance with an initial small request in order to facilitate compliance with subsequent larger requests."[43] Understanding that this technique can be successful, the influence operator must develop not only the first step but also the subsequent incremental steps that will follow. Crucial to this technique is knowing the target audience's perspective on the issue, and just how much variance can be incorporated into the subsequent steps moving toward the desired end state. Scott concluded that this "may be more effective than traditional persuasive appeals in mass communication settings where personal contact is not possible."[44] Thus this technique has applicability to the Army's efforts at the strategic and operational levels, which lack the opportunity for many personal contacts for carrying the message to a large audience across a nation or region.

Cognitive dissonance theory explains the need for an individual to maintain cognitive consistency. Under the theory of societal norm messaging, influence operators ought to take dissonance theory into consideration. The application of dissonance theory looks at a target audience's need to execute expected actions and suggests that without maintaining these actions internal turmoil occurs at the individual level. An example of dissonance theory within a society is "when a society honors the social norm to help the less fortunate, the person internalizes the norm, and failing to help [the less fortunate], can induce feelings of guilt."[45] This suggests other techniques for persuasion, such as guilt appeals. The linkage between techniques, target audience analysis, and analysis of the larger environment can reveal particular pressure points that techniques

13

such as guilt appeals may be applied against. The guilt appeals may be beneficial if the societal norm is understood, and using guilt appeals may influence a particular target audience to alter their behavior toward the existing societal norm.

Expectancy Violation Theory (EVT) is another potential theory for consideration. EVT is useful for understanding a target audience's perception of an issue, and helpful in determining whether to use statistical data as part of the message. However, before explaining how EVT relates to influence operations, it is important to understand the concept of "framing."

The dictionary defines frame as "[to] express something in a particular way or construct an idea or statement."[46] George Lakoff gives the influence field a more appropriate definition in his book *Don't Think of an Elephant*, where he defines frames as "mental structures that shape the way we see the world."[47] Just as the concept of framing is essential for influence operators to understand, so too is Expectancy Violation Theory, which can be defined as when an individual's frame of the issue is different from the actual.

It is when the influence operator should take EVT and framing into account in message design that connects the two. Whether or not the use of statistical data will be successful in shifting the target audience's behavior also connects the two. Campo found that when statistical data used in a message caused a negative expectation violation, i.e. the statistical data was too different from what the receiver perceived (and therefore expected), the target audience's judgment might change but the behavior commonly did not. [48] Although Campo's study, *Social Norms and Expectancy Violation,* found that "social norms may work to change judgments but do not result in consistent attitude change" and "judgment change is not the main cause of attitude change upon receipt of a social norm message, particularly when the message is contrary to what the target audience observes in their society,"[49]considering social norms and addressing the possibility of drawing attention in order to change toward a more accepted international norm should be part of the influence operator's calculation.

Campo's study is referenced in order to make it clear that while social norm marketing may not result in changing behaviors, it may still prove useful in adjusting attitudes, which can be the first step towards eventual behavioral modification. A good example of an attempted norming message failing based on social norm expectation was the United Kingdom's campaign to discourage binge drinking and set what the government viewed as acceptable levels for drinking. The campaign used a negative approach in their messages to convey what would happen as a result of binge drinking: for example one drunken teen falling to his death during an inebriated stunt. The drastic examples provided, of horrible results occurring if individuals typically drank above the recommended levels, did not resonate. These messages were not reinforced through other observations by the target audience, such as their continuous observation of elders drinking heavily over the years with no apparent effect.[50] In this case the UK government attempted to adjust a social norm by providing selected statistical data. However, because the product/s were based on poor target audience analysis, mirror-imaging, and failing to craft a message that fit within the reality of expectation of the target audience, (as it exists in the minds of the target audience), resulted in an unbelievable message. When the message exceeds the realm of the possible for the target audience, then it and subsequent messages will be rejected.

There is also a need to understand the context in which the social issue targeted for change is embedded, because how it is viewed culturally may have a dramatic impact on the ability to change the societal viewpoint of the issue. A well researched target audience analysis will provide better insight than relying on the "marketer's [or influence operator's] perception of a moral dilemma and his or her socio-cultural frame of reference"[51]

Applying the understanding of theory, a detailed analysis, and associated techniques also helps to prevent influence operators from addressing the solution to an issue through a "foreign lens" perspective, also called mirror-imaging. Mirror-imaging is the internalized assumption, by the influence operator, that the target audience will respond in similar fashion to members of the influence operator's own society. Knowing more about the target audience, their environment, and society, will greatly facilitate development of messages and actions without this error built in. Techniques that may work in the influence operator's society may not work in the target audience's society, based solely on the fact the target audience does not share the same societal or cultural norms and assumptions prerequisite for that technique to work. An example of mirror-imaging is that the USG expects the North Korean leadership to respond to U.S. led pressure or actions against the North Korean nuclear program in a manner similar to the way the USG would respond if faced with the same pressures. Influence operators must be aware of their human tendency to apply foreign lens or mirror-imaging to situations. They should instead rely on theory, analysis, and proven techniques to avoid missteps.

Agenda setting theory looks at what the media provides the public. It was initially developed out of research on the public's response to media coverage during political campaigns: when the media defines the important issues, what is the corresponding emphasis that voters subsequently place on those same issues? "Agenda setting refers to the idea that there is a strong correlation between the emphasis that mass media places on certain issues and the importance attributed to these issues by mass audiences. (McCombs & Shaw, 1972)"[52] "The general notion of agenda-setting [is] the ability of the media to influence the salience of events in the public mind."[53] McCombs and Shaw make the point that through mass communication the media does not necessarily attempt to tell the public how to think on an issue, but rather what issues to think about.

At the strategic and operational levels, this may be extremely helpful in developing an influence campaign across a region with diverse audiences when attempting to focus them on a particular issue. Separately inserting products applying appropriate message design will provide our desired input concerning issues for the public agenda. Understanding how this theory works would be useful to influence efforts. In other words, influence operators can attempt to drive the topics through their messages, crafting the messages in order to solicit dialogue on particular issues and simultaneously, through supporting and other media, providing their interpretation of how the issue should be perceived or resolved. The supplemented messages from multiple sources, i.e. television, radio, print, key leader engagements, etc., help not only to get the issue on the target audience's agenda of what to think about, it also presents messages favorable to the originator's point of view.

The third significant finding from the study had to do with the fundamentals of campaign design. Gantz studied the impact of mass media on increasing the behavior of using seat belts. Gantz first insisted, "media campaigns often appear to be far more successful in conveying information and changing attitudes than in altering behaviors."[54] However, he also attested that many times the reason for shortcomings in campaign effects were due to either poor execution of the development process or components of the process being missed. One very useful assertion near the end of the study was that "[b]ehavioral changes such as [increasing seat-belt use] demand long-term, high frequency, multimedia campaigns."[55] The correlation to our purpose is that when we are attempting to change a long held behavior or cultural practice, even one that has self-preservation as a central point, a prolonged media campaign may be required. Although current doctrine[56] provides programs and series as a means to reinforce a message sequentially over time, it falls short in developing a phased campaign effort with explanations of establishing conditions that, when observed in the target audience, would be the cue to move to the next message and/or subsequent phase.

Personal experience has convinced me of the need to implement campaign phasing in order for communication efforts to succeed. By virtue of commanding two different task forces in two different wars (OIF and OEF) for a total of 24 months, each of whose primary objective was to influence target audiences at the strategic and operational levels, I found developing a phased communication campaign is necessary to achieve the desired behavioral effect when that desired behavior constitutes a significant paradigm shift.

Many times we were working to shift a paradigm, especially at the strategic or operational levels. The process of developing the individual products, as discussed above, is executed inside the communication campaign. Multiple products were then linked as a series that hopefully pushed the audience towards the desired behavior. Doctrinally this is referred to as a series of products. However, it is important to understand that one or two products cannot by themselves shift an entire paradigm. Further, this may not be achieved in a matter of weeks or months. This may actually take a steady drumbeat of messaging over an extended period of time, possibly even years. The most significant takeaway was the need to identify the desired end behavior of the target audience from the beginning, i.e. active participation in the democratic process, or stopping support to terrorist activities, and the evolutionary steps the target audience needed to take toward ultimately changing their behavior.

Once the desired behavioral effect was determined, the designer developed a sequence of messages along a phased campaign. Key to current and subsequent messaging was timing the dissemination of the subsequent messages. The conditions the cognitive state of the target audience had to meet were identified before moving to the subsequent phase or message. In order to achieve the correct timing for introducing the subsequent message, assessments of the effort would need to confirm that the cognitive conditions in the target audience had at each stage changed sufficiently. That next incremental message had to be reasonably within reach of the target audience's frame, or not exceed the parameters as referenced in the earlier discussions of expectancy violation theory. By virtue of developing this detailed line of messaging along a supported line of operation,[57] the influence operator can apply the theory and differing techniques to gradually shift the paradigm of the target audience. Rimer discussed a similar approach when addressing tailored health communications. She discussed the importance of "disaggregat[ing] key steps in the behavior change process, for example, reception, acceptance, yielding, and impact."[58] An understanding of the behavioral change process or behavioral pathway may serve as a template to develop each phase and the cognitive conditions of a target audience associated within a phased communication campaign.

The fourth significant finding of this study was in regards to understanding message credibility. Message credibility is not only dependent on the designed message's wording, but also on the source disseminating the message. When dealing with foreign audiences it is better to consider providing the message from a source that will be viewed as credible by that audience. The State Department's *Shared Values Initiative* program sought to provide Muslim audiences around the world insight on what life was like in America for Muslims. Kendrick's[59] study revealed "the one-sided nature of the videos appeared to play a large role in the credibility of the overall message." As such, when the provenance of the message was known or assumed to be USG, because of the obviously favorable representation of America in the text or branding that clearly stated USG as the source, the message is further scrutinized by the receiving audience. However, "propaganda literature suggests that a two-sided message serves to inoculate the recipient against future counterarguments and is more likely to persuade an educated audience (Lowery and DeFleur, 1995)."[60] To achieve or maintain credibility of messages, it is often necessary to present a moderate view instead of solely presenting the originator's view. Even though the actual message being provided by the USG may be factual and credible, it can quickly be tainted and viewed as suspicious if seen as coming directly from a USG sponsored source. Therefore, it may be necessary to utilize another means for the message to be disseminated so as not to taint the target audience's perception of the message before they process it.

The source of message dissemination should also be a focus of the target audience analysis. Understanding the importance of achieving and maintaining message credibility throughout the process of message design and application helps to maintain credibility of the entire messaging effort. Incremental messaging achieves more towards convincing the target audience in the overall effort for the long run. Influence operators cannot allow themselves, or be forced to create a haphazard message that is so far outside the frame of the target audience that it will likely be discounted, thereby lacking any credibility. By providing an incremental, steady drumbeat of credible messages, an influence campaign will build a convincing argument with each message and ultimately produce results.

Future research

There is one area suggested for future research from which the military influence community would benefit. The U.S. military has sought to implement an accurate, objective, credible means of assessing influence efforts over the past two decades, but particularly in the last 12 years. The same issue that plagues health related communication campaigns also affects military influence campaigns, and that is the ability to accurately assess whether the money, time, and actions committed resulted in the desired behavioral change. Noar's conclusion that "the fact that many campaigns are executed in entire regions or countries and as such do[es] not lend themselves to

21

randomized controlled designs (Do & Kincaid, 2006; Hornik, 2002; Pettifor et al., 2007)" [61] describes the same problem faced by strategic and operational influence campaigns.

Current doctrine includes the step of assessment. The process, described earlier by Noar, also has an assessment step as well. Step 7, *Outcome Evaluation*, is a vital part of every effort and a necessity in every communication or influence campaign. Whether from the commercial perspective, determining if marketing and advertising efforts resulted in increased profit margin, or in political and military use, determining whether target audiences moved towards a desired behavior, evaluation of efforts provides the all important feedback on whether the campaign achieved its intended impact.

This study identified some of the common techniques of evaluation such as pre- and post-test designs, post-test only designs, or control group designs. Although previous research had indicated, as expected, that it was easier to measure knowledge and attitude, with behavioral tests being less common,[62] recent evidence suggests that well managed campaigns can achieve "demonstrated effects on behavior or behavioral intentions."[63] This suggests that following prescribed steps of campaign design and clearly developing outcome evaluations including measures of behavior can show results.[64] Conducting the evaluation is often the most difficult step to implement, but a necessary step nonetheless.

Additionally, due to the way budget monies are allocated to the U.S. military, there are requirements to provide assessments on what has been spent and achieved during the annual funding period. Future research is needed on how best to assess the effect of influence operations. It will likely be through long-term evaluation of any desired effect. In order to conduct these evaluations, one would first need to determine a reasonable timeframe for indicators, the desired behavior changes, and what would reasonably count as manifestations that the behaviors might be changing. In other words, research should consider measuring correlation versus causation, since rarely are communication efforts the sole reason for behavioral change. Habitually, communication is but one factor among many that influence; just as stated in the draft definition of *Human Domain*. Despite understanding that influence operations are just one factor contributing to change, Influence Operators are often tasked with the possibly unachievable requirement of quantifying the actual changes that have occurred strictly as a result of their messaging efforts. This, as Noar stated, is nearly impossible, but it is something that should be looked at in further research to provide a manageable means to evaluate outcome of influence efforts, even if from a "logical objective correlation" viewpoint.

I use the term *logical objective correlation* as a means to define through wording the intent of an influence assessment. As Noar asserted, the difficulty in assessing communication efforts and the difficulty faced when attempting to collect on a broad scale effort among foreign cultures within a confined time frame (annually), the assessment may benefit by looking at the change of perceptions over a greater timeframe with a logical interpretation of past or current events, information, or intelligence regarding the target audience's changing perceptions. These observations must be objective so as not to read into events the desired outcome or interpretation.

Thus, these should be viewed as a correlation. While causational changes are most preferred and provide the greatest legitimacy towards an assessment, they are rare and even then can typically be questionable because of the vast amount of other factors that impact target audience's perceptions. Causational linkage is especially expected by those outside the field of influence who think they understand, but typically only have had the opportunity to question efforts vice actually executing them on the ground. Determining possible correlation between messaging and behavioral changes is much more realistic and timely.

Conclusions and Recommendations for the Army

As the Army looks toward the future and toward engaging in the Human Domain, there is merit to looking at empirical data from the academic literature on how the Human Domain may be influenced in the psychological environment. This research has provided an important step forward regarding the types of insights available. Specifically two significant results have come to the forefront in terms of relevance to U.S. Army influence operations.

The first recommendation for the U.S. Army in the body of research is to increase the study of behavioral theory and techniques, and add a step to the current doctrinal process of *Identify behavioral theory or theories to be used.* To develop an effective influence design, the foundation of the approach should be developed based upon solid behavioral and message design theory. Academe is constantly developing, researching, and providing research results regarding behavioral theory and message design. Many of the theories outlined in this research could provide an enhanced capability for USG efforts across the globe. Identifying a proven theory at the beginning of the influence process is sound practice and as such should be implemented as a specified step to ensure the process remains current, credible, and validated in proven research. The community of influence operators should put in place a means to constantly review new reports, as well as engage with academic centers of excellence regarding new theories and practices. Only through such engagement and consistent diligence to find what works, will the influence profession progress and its' processes improve.

Secondly, there is a need to include communication campaign design and phasing into influence instruction. The influence community needs to add the instruction of phased communication effort development, with conditions, in support of the military campaign line of operation. Shifting target audience behavioral paradigms is not a rapid process. Influence operators applying a detailed target audience analysis with solid behavioral theory over a phased construct, coupled with an assessment mechanism to identify the presence of cognitive conditions, will provide a greater potential for success. Implementation of these recommendations will significantly enhance the capabilities of the U.S. Army influence operators at the strategic and operational levels.

## Endnotes

[1] Greg Jaffe, "U.S. model for a future war fans tensions with China and inside Pentagon," August 1, 2012, linked from *The Washington Post Home Page* at "National Security," http://www.washingtonpost.com/world/national-security/us-model-for-a-future-war-fans-tensions-with-china-and-inside-pentagon/2012/08/01/gJQAC6F8PX_story.html (accessed April 12, 2013); U.S. Joint Chiefs of Staff, *Joint Operational Access Concept* (JOAC) Version 1.0, (Washington, DC: U.S. Joint Chiefs of Staff, January 17, 2012): 4.

[2] Kristina Wong, "Gen. Martin Dempsey: Pentagon reassessing defense strategy under sequestration," March 14, 2013, linked from *The Washington Times Home Page* at "Security," http://www.washingtontimes.com/news/2013/mar/14/gen-martin-dempsey-pentagon-reassessing-defense-st/ (accessed March 22, 2013).

³ Ibid.

⁴ Richard Sisk, "'Human Domain' Enters Future Army War Plans," February 20, 2013, linked from *Military.com* Home Page at "News," www.military.com/dailynews/2013/02/20/human-domain-enters-future-army-war-plans.html (accessed February 21, 2013).

⁵ Ibid.

⁶ Ibid.

⁷ Pre-decisional draft documents staffing draft (Version 0.8) of the Army Functional Concept for the 7ᵗʰ Warfighting Function (March 2013).

⁸ U.S. Joint Chiefs of Staff, *Capstone Construct for Joint Operations: Joint Force 2020*, (Washington, DC: U.S. Joint Chiefs of Staff, September 10, 2012), www.dtic.mil/future**joint**warfare/**concepts**/ccjo_2012.pdf, (accessed April 11, 2013).

⁹ Justin Tang, "Leaders emphasize importance of human domain as Army plans for future," March 28, 2013, linked from *The United States Army Home Page* at "News Archives," http://www.army.mil/article/99772/ (accessed April 11, 2013).

¹⁰ General Raymond T. Odierno, Chief of Staff of the Army, "CSA editorial: Prevent, shape, win," December 16, 2011, linked from *The United States Army Home Page* at "News Archives," http://www.army.mil/article/71030 (accessed March 21, 2013).

¹¹ This is discussed at length in several volumes of work to include: Ricks, Thomas E. 2012, *The Generals*, Penguin Group, New York.  and  John A. Nagl, 2002. *Counterinsurgency lessons from Malaya to Vietnam: Learning to eat soup with a knife,* Greenwood Publishing, Westport.

¹² U.S. Department of the Army, *Counter-insurgency Operations*, Field Manual 3-24 (Washington, DC: U.S. Department of the Army, December 2006).

¹³ Brown, Robert B. Major General (USA) and MAJ Ronald W. Sprang, "Human Domain: Essential to victory in future operations," no date available:1.

¹⁴ Ibid., 6.

¹⁵ U.S. Joint Chiefs of Staff, *Joint Intelligence,* Joint Publication 2-0, (Washington, DC: U.S. Joint Chiefs of Staff, June 22, 2007): GL-10.

¹⁶ For the purposes of this paper, "influence operators" is defined as those individuals operating in units or serving on staffs involved in planning and executing actions specifically designed to influence the perceptions and subsequent behavior of a target audience. U.S. Department of the Army, *Special Operations*, Army Doctrine Reference Publication 3-05, (Washington, DC: U.S. Department of the Army, August 31, 2012): 2-7.

[17] U.S. Department of the Army, *Psychological Operations Process Tactics, Techniques, and Procedures*, Field Manual 3-05.301 (Washington, DC: U.S. Department of the Army, August 2007).

[18] A "product" is the actual medium the selected message is place onto. It is a culmination of extracting information from the target audience analysis and delivering the intended message from a determined theme. Examples of products are a loudspeaker message, leaflet, handbill, radio message, radio program, television commercial, documentary, etc. After development and testing of the product, it is then disseminated via a media such as face to face communications, radio, television, etc.

[19] U.S. Department of the Army, *Psychological Operations Process Tactics, Techniques, and Procedures*, ix.

[20] Ibid.

[21] Ibid., vii.

[22] Numerous keyword searches were used in the search, including influence, attitude, persuasion, campaign, marketing, advertising, social change, social norm, behavior, and effectiveness.

[23] Based on personal experience, Demand Reduction was one of the focus areas of the U.S. Office of National Drug Control Policy (ONDCP) and addressed by U.S. military elements in deployed areas. Some areas addressed were eradication and alternative development. www.whitehouse.gov/ondcp

[24] The "RACE" model is used in Public Relations. RACE is an acronym for Research, Action Planning, Communication, and Evaluation. The RACE serves as a means to specify steps for a public relations campaign. Each letter in the acronym is then broken down into sub-steps.

[25] Rimer, Barbara, and Matthew W. Kreuter. 2006. "Advancing Tailored Health Communication: A Persuasion and Message Effects Perspective." *Journal of Communications* 56: S184-S201. Communication & Mass Media Complete, EBSCOhost (accessed November 8, 2012): 189.

[26] Noar, Seth M. , Philip Palmgreen, Melissa Chabot, Nicole Dobransky, and Rick S. Zimmerman. 2009. "A 10 year systematic review of HIV/AIDS Mass Communication Campaigns: Have we made progress?" *Journal of Health Communication* 14, no. 1: 15-42. Communication & Mass Media Complete, EBSCOhost (accessed October 4, 2012)

[27] Herbert Hoover and Hugh Gibson, *The Problems of Lasting Peace* (Doran and Company: Doubleday Publishing, 1942): 2.

[28] Outcome expectancies are beliefs about the consequences of performing the behavior. Fishbein, Martin., Kathleen Hall-Jamieson, Eric Zimmer, Ina Von Haeften and Robin Nabi. 2002. "Avoiding the Boomerang: Testing the Relative Effectiveness of Anti-drug Public Service Announcements before a National Campaign." *American Journal of Public Health* 92, no. 2: 238-245. Academic Search Complete, EBSCOhost (accessed September 24, 2012): 238.

[29] Ibid., Normative beliefs are beliefs about the behaviors and normative proscriptions of relevant others.

[30] Ibid., Self-efficacy beliefs are beliefs that one can perform the behavior, even under a number of difficult conditions.

[31] Ibid., 239.

[32] Fishbein, "Avoiding the Boomerang"; Campo, Shelly., Dominique Brossard, M. Somjen Frazer, Timothy Marchell, Deborah Lewis, and Janis Talbot. 2004. "Social Norms and Expectancy Violation Theories:  Assessing the effectiveness of health communication campaigns." *Communication Monographs* 71, no. 4: 481-498. Communication & Mass Media Complete, EBSCOhost (accessed September 22, 2012); Scott, Carol A. 1977. "Modifying Socially-Conscious Behavior: The Foot-in-the-Door Technique." *Journal of Consumer Research* 4, no. 3: 156-164. Business Source  Complete, EBSCOhost (accessed November 4, 2012); Thomas Risse, Steven Ropp, and Kathryn Sikkink, *The Power of Human Rights: International Norms and Domestic Change.* (Cambridge, UK: Cambridge University Press, 1999).

[33] Noar, "A 10 year systematic review," 37.

[34] Ibid., 16. The seven steps are (1) conducting formative research on and about the target audience, (2) using theory as a conceptual foundation, (3) segmenting one's audience into meaningful subgroups, (4) using a message design approach that is targeted to the audience segments, (5) utilizing effective channels widely viewed by and persuasive with the target audience, (6) conducting process evaluation and ensuring high message exposure, and (7) using a sensitive outcome evaluation design that reduces threats to internal validity and allows casual inferences about campaign impact to be made.

[35] Ibid.

[36] Ibid., 31.

[37] Social norms are those beliefs and perceptions already held by a member of that society as an accepted view.  These beliefs and perceptions are often not questioned until presented with an outside perspective.

[38] Campo, Shelly., Dominique Brossard, M. Somjen Frazer, Timothy Marchell, Deborah Lewis, and Janis Talbot. 2004. "Social Norms and Expectancy Violation Theories:  Assessing the effectiveness of health communication campaigns." *Communication Monographs* 71, no. 4: 481-498. Communication & Mass Media Complete, EBSCOhost (accessed September 22, 2012): 449.

[39] Kelley, Judith, and Beth A. Simmons. 2012. "From Scrutiny to Shame: Information as Social Pressure in International Relations." manuscript draft (unpublished): 29.

[40] Nadelman, Ethan A. "Global Prohibition Regimes: The Evolution of Norms in International Society." *International Organization* 44, no. 4,(1990). JSTOR, (accessed February 10, 2013): 496.

[41] Bem, Daryl J., 1972. "Self-Perception Theory." *Advances in experimental social psychology*, volume 6, Academic Press, Inc. New York and London. Google Scholar (accessed March 24, 2013) (www.dbem.ws/SPTheory.pdf).

[42] Scott, Carol A. 1977. "Modifying Socially-Conscious Behavior: The Foot-in-the-Door Technique." *Journal of Consumer Research* 4, no. 3: 156-164. Business Source Complete, EBSCOhost (accessed November 4, 2012): 157.

[43] Ibid., 156.

[44] Ibid., 163.

[45] Chang, Chun-Tuan. 2011. "Guilt appeals in cause-related marketing." *International Journal of Advertising* 30, no. 4: 587-616. Business Source Complete, EBSCOhost (accessed November 4, 2012): 589.

[46] Microsoft Encarta dictionary, Microsoft reference tools

[47] Lakoff, George., *Don't Think of an Elephant! Know Your Values and Frame the Debate*, Chelsea Green Publishing, White River Junction, 2004, p. xv.

[48] Campo, "Social Norms," 467.

[49] Ibid.

[50] Szmigin, Isabelle, Andrew Bengry-Howell, Christine Griffin, Chris Hackley, Willm Mistral. 2011. "Social marketing, individual responsibility and the culture of intoxication." *European Journal of Marketing* 45, no. 5: 759-779. PsycINFO, EBSCOhost (accessed September 22, 2012): 775.

[51] Ibid., 761.

[52] Scheufele, Dietram A., and David Tewksbury. 2007. "Framing, Agenda Setting, and Priming: The Evolution of Three Media Effects Models." *Journal of Communication* 57, no. 1: 9-20. *Communication & Mass Media Complete*, EBSCO*host* (accessed April 12, 2013):11.

[53] Shaw, Donald L., and Maxwell E. McCombs, *The Emergence of American Political Issues: The Agenda Setting Function of the Press*, West Publishing, St. Paul, 1977: 5.

[54] Gantz, Walter, Michael Fitzmaurice, Euisun Yoo. 1990. "Seat belt Campaigns and buckling up: Do the Media make a difference?" *Health Communication* 2, no. 1: 1-12. Communication and Mass Media Complete, EBSCOhost (accessed November 4, 2012): 2.

[55] Ibid., 11.

[56] U.S. Department of the Army, *Psychological Operations Process Tactics, Techniques, and Procedures.*

[57] Line of operation is a line that defines the directional orientation of a force in time and space in relation to the enemy and links the force with its base of operations and objectives.

U.S. Department of the Army, *Operational Terms and Military Symbols*, Army Doctrine Reference Publication 1-02, C2, (Washington, DC: U.S. Department of the Army, November 28, 2012).

[58] Rimer, "Advancing Tailored Health Communication," 191.

[59] Kendrick, Alice, and Jami A. Fullerton. 2004. "Advertising as Public Diplomacy: Attitude Change among International Audiences" *Journal of Advertising Research* 44, no. 3: 297-311. Communication & Mass Media Complete, EBSCOhost (accessed October 4, 2012): 309.

[60] Ibid.

[61] Noar,"*A 10 year systematic review,*" 36.

[62] Ibid., 34.

[63] Ibid., 35.

[64] Ibid.

www.ingramcontent.com/pod-product-compliance
Lightning Source LLC
Chambersburg PA
CBHW080753290526
45790CB00008B/3427